THE ABUNDANCE OF WEALTH™

Receive the gifts of prosperity.

Understand the energy and flow of prosperity
and weave the threads of abundance throughout the tapestry of your life.

THE ABUNDANCE OF WEALTH COPYRIGHT

Copyright © 2010-2013 by Miranda J. Barrett.
Original Concept Copyright © 2008 by Miranda J. Barrett.
Copyright © 2010 Front Cover Artwork by Helena Nelson-Reed.

All rights reserved. This book may not be reproduced in whole or in part without written permission. In accordance with the U.S. Copyright act of 1976, the scanning, uploading and electronic sharing of any part of this book without permission of the publisher is unlawful piracy and theft of the author's intellectual property.

If you would like to use material from the book (other than for review purposes), prior written permission must be obtained by contacting either the publisher at:

Info@MirandaJBarrett.com
or the artist at www.HelenaNelsonReed.com
Thank you for the support of the author and the artist's rights.

please note:

The written or spoken information, ideas, procedures and suggestions contained and presented in 'THE ABUNDANCE OF WEALTH' workshops and books are meant for educational purposes only and are not for diagnosis. It should not be used as a substitute for your physician's advice. 'THE ABUNDANCE OF WEALTH' is not therapy and is not intended to replace the recommendations of a licensed health practitioner. It is the responsibility of the reader to consult with their own medical Doctor, Counselor, Therapist or other competent professional regarding any condition before adopting any of the suggestions in this book.

THE ABUNDANCE OF WEALTH™

Dedicated to the inner flow of abundance, which resides within us and to the well of gratitude where prosperity is birthed.

MISSION STATEMENT

To guide and facilitate women
in becoming their most beautiful and radiant selves.

To acknowledge and embrace the well of love
and power which lies within all women and to ignite the
awakening and embodying of this life force.

To empower each woman, through exquisite self-care and love,
to live her fullest life possible, and to walk her path of wisdom
and truth, as she shares this light and knowledge
with all beings.

IN DEEP GRATITUDE
Thank you

The creation, birth and life of 'A Woman's Truth' would not have been possible without the love, support and devotion from the following angels in my life:

My beautiful daughter Megan who naturally embodies the teachings of living in her truth and integrity, thank you for the creative gift of the beautiful artwork. Helena Nelson-Reed for her generosity of spirit in allowing her extraordinary artwork, which embodies the teachings so magnificently, to grace the covers. Dennise Marie Keller for her unwavering support and dedication to the teachings and for proofing, editing, aligning and translating my vision into the technical world of manifestation. Dan Fowler for his creative genius and dedication. Lucy Alexander and Suzanne Ryan, my dearest friends for their amazing editing and wholehearted encouragement. Monica Marsh for her commitment, support and belief in the workshops. Maggie Crawford, my mum, for her proofing and for being a living example of the teachings. Cait Myer and Katie Steen for their patience and ability to decipher my handwriting and for formatting the books. Bethany Kelly for her support. Deborah Waring for holding the space for the conception of 'A Woman's Truth' to be born and for her insight in the first year of teaching and Emmanuel for believing in my vision.

My mentors and teachers Rod Stryker, Adyashanti and Alison Armstrong, Max Simon and Jeffrey Van Dyk for their continuous and guiding light in my life, their never-ending belief in my potential and for always teaching me the way to evolve into my highest and most potent self. And to all of you beautiful and courageous women who are committing to living your truth and transforming into your most radiant selves,

thank you.

A PRELUDE

An overture to the abundance of wealth.

All of us have the capacity to lead a life full of blessing. 'The Abundance of Wealth' provides insightful wisdom and practical exercises to help enjoy a life of true wealth. This book will guide you in assessing your inner state, monitoring your outward behavior and acting in order to realize your full potential.

In my own life, I have found that to become personally abundant requires many commitments. One must set goals, create a written plan, work hard to implement this plan and constantly adjust and improve one's strategy. In order to begin this process one must be filled with an inner sense of power and a belief that one can actually command one's destiny. One must be filled with faith, a belief that the universe is full of abundance and blessings to be continually received and shared.

I have found that it is vitally important to use affirmations to program the brain for success. My favorite over the years has been, "I happily earn _____ dollars a year!" I have also experienced that the more one gives to others the more one receives. 'The Abundance of Wealth' will be a helpful tool to anyone who chooses to implement this program!

Miranda is a gifted healer. Her insights are invaluable and help me to keep centered on the important rather than the urgent. Her intuition is very accurate and the simple teachings within this book will support and align you in receiving the wealth and abundance you so deserve.

~ Robert Floe
President and Founder of Floe Financial Partners

I'm not an expert on money matters but I am well versed in the energy of money. I have been a long-time client of Miranda's and during my first session with her, she was checking out my energy fields. During that session she assessed my money field was in good shape. She did not know anything about me during that first meeting and I knew nothing about her but I could tell she knew what she was talking about in concept. She was right on! My money fields are in good shape and I really could not ask for more. However, this was not always the case.

I grew up poor. Not like the streets of India poor but with the innate understanding that we had less than other people do. I knew not to ask my "Single-hardworking-Mom" for anything when we went to the supermarket. It would only upset her that she could not afford to buy us the "name brand" cereal that I had seen on TV. I wore my brother's hand-me-downs. We often ate Peas and Rice for dinner. Sometimes I would even "forget" my lunch because the lunch that was provided at school was more interesting than mine was.

Therefore, as a young child I developed an ability to conjure money. I was aware that it was everywhere and I would seek it out. I would find money constantly. A few dollars here, $50 there would show up. I would turn my attention to the ground and it would appear. My Mother thought I might be stealing because it happened so often. She began to rely on it. I remember crossing the Golden Gate Bridge and we had a toll to pay. Once again, she had no money but casually asked me, sitting in the back seat of her car, if I had any? I handed over a $20.00 that I had stuffed in my pocket. I was 10 and bummed because she kept the change.

By watching my mother struggle with money issues, it helped me to develop my own belief system. It was as if her inability to manage money created my desire to embrace it. To focus positively on the freedom of having money and not the lack there of, I created it. I worked hard and I respected money. I was not "too good" to pick up a shiny penny. I was not careless or stingy. As a freelance Fashion Stylist, I would never turn down a job even if it paid less than my "usual" day rate. Money was Money. I knew that it was all a matter of flow. I put my positive energies forth and it comes to me. In addition, I am truly grateful for the ease and grace in which I can live my life now. Moreover, Miranda can show you the way.

~ Rene Chiara
Freelance Fashion Stylist

THE ABUNDANCE OF WEALTH™

Gems of Love

THE ABUNDANCE OF WEALTH	1
THE ABUNDANCE OF MONEY	4
FOR THE LOVE OF MONEY	10
GRATITUDE IN THE LAND OF PLENTY	12
THE ILLUSION OF MONEY	19
UNVEIL YOUR MONEY RELATIONSHIP	20
THE BONDAGE OF MONEY	24
MONEY AND SELF WORTH	26
MONEY AND EMOTIONS	28
THE BOND OF MONEY AND FEAR	30
YOUR PARTNERSHIP WITH MONEY	34
A TRICK TO MONEY IS HAVING SOME	36
IN WHAT DO YOU INVEST?	39
NOTHING IS FOR FREE	42
GIVING	45
GIVING UP	48

INCOME VERSUS OUTCOME 51

SAVING MONEY 54

RETIREMENT AND THE GOLDEN YEARS 58

THE BIGGEST GIFT OF DEATH 61

MONEY SAVING TIPS 65

DEBT IS A FOUR LETTER WORD 68

F**K YOU MONEY 71

EXPAND MONEY CONSCIOUSNESS 72

DOUBLE YOUR MONEY 74

DOUBLE YOUR MONEY DIARY 77

THE MONEY POT 78

REVEAL MORE TRUTH 81

THE HAPPINESS EQUATION 83

CHARTS, CHARTS, GLORIOUS CHARTS 84

A REVEALING MONEY CHART 85

You can download a copy of the **Money Chart and the Happiness Equation**
from Miranda's website at:

www.MirandaJBarrett.com/resources/the-abundance-of-wealth

A DAILY PRACTICE
Commit to Yourself

*F*ollow these simple steps daily as a way to instill and strengthen your heartfelt resolve to love yourself. This will help to keep you aligned, transforming and on track, giving you a stable foundation for the rest of your life. As a gift to yourself, please mark the teachings as you read them through and congratulate yourself with each one. See each day as a commitment to take exquisite care of yourself.

- ◊ DAY ONE: THE ABUNDANCE OF WEALTH 2
- ◊ DAY TWO: THE ABUNDANCE OF MONEY 4
- ◊ DAY THREE: FOR THE LOVE OF MONEY 10
- ◊ DAY FOUR: GRATITUDE IN THE LAND OF PLENTY 12
- ◊ DAY FIVE: THE ILLUSION OF MONEY 19
- ◊ DAY SIX: UNVEIL YOUR MONEY RELATIONSHIP 20
- ◊ DAY SEVEN: THE BONDAGE OF MONEY 24
- ◊ DAY EIGHT: MONEY AND SELF WORTH 26
- ◊ DAY NINE: MONEY AND EMOTIONS 28
- ◊ DAY TEN: THE BOND OF MONEY AND FEAR 30
- ◊ DAY ELEVEN: YOUR PARTNERSHIP WITH MONEY 34
- ◊ DAY TWELVE: A TRICK TO MONEY IS HAVING SOME 36
- ◊ DAY THIRTEEN: IN WHAT DO YOU INVEST? 39
- ◊ DAY FOURTEEN: NOTHING IS FOR FREE 42
- ◊ DAY FIFTEEN: GIVING 45

- ◊ DAY SIXTEEN: GIVING UP 48
- ◊ DAY SEVENTEEN: INCOME VERSUS OUTCOME 51
- ◊ DAY EIGHTEEN: SAVING MONEY 54
- ◊ DAY NINTEEN: RETIREMENT AND THE GOLDEN YEARS 58
- ◊ DAY TWENTY: THE BIGGEST GIFT OF DEATH 61
- ◊ DAY TWENTY-ONE: MONEY SAVING TIPS 65
- ◊ DAY TWENTY-TWO: DEBT IS A FOUR LETTER WORD 68
- ◊ DAY TWENTY-THREE: F**K YOU MONEY 71
- ◊ DAY TWENTY-FOUR: EXPAND MONEY CONSCIOUSNESS 72
- ◊ DAY TWENTY-FIVE: DOUBLE YOUR MONEY 74
- ◊ DAY TWENTY-SIX: DOUBLE YOUR MONEY DIARY 77
- ◊ DAY TWENTY-SEVEN: THE MONEY POT 78
- ◊ DAY TWENTY-EIGHT: REVEAL MORE TRUTH 81
- ◊ DAY TWENTY-NINE: THE HAPPINESS EQUATION 83
- ◊ DAY THIRTY: CHART, CHARTS, GLORIOUS CHARTS 84
- ◊ EVERYDAY: A REVEALING MONEY CHART 85

You can download a copy of the **Money Chart and the Happiness Equation**

from Miranda's website at:

www.MirandaJBarrett.com/resources/the-abundance-of-wealth

A LIFE WORTH LIVING

"Never give from your well.
Always give from your overflow."
~ Rumi

All too often as women, your own needs are denied for the benefit of others as you orchestrate your life through demands and expectations you feel responsible for. Unfortunately, this can leave you without the juice and energy needed to be present fully and to enjoy life. During these readings, you will continually discover more about who you truly are and learn the tools needed to live your most authentic and fulfilling life possible. From this place, you will experience being 'full to overflowing' and all the joy and energy this brings.

As you delve into these teachings, you will explore, laugh, study, share, and freely express who you are. In this sacred space, you will ultimately learn your truth as a woman in order to shine, to embody your own beauty, believe in your own worth, and take exquisite care of yourself. For only in this way can you truly be of service.

During these guidebooks, many of the basic needs of women will be explored such as sleep, nutrition, creativity, movement and time to replenish. A topic has been chosen for each book and a cohesive and practical foundation is laid out to inspire and guide you. This will bring about a new strength and resolve which will allow your needs to become a priority, without letting your outer world dictate otherwise. By the end of our time together, the concept of being confident, loving, serene and passionate will no longer be a distant fantasy. Instead, these and many other extraordinary qualities that you naturally embody as a woman will flow with ease, grace and love.

With life's demands so high, it has become imperative that your needs are first acknowledged, honored and then taken care of. From this vantage point, your relationship with yourself then has the potential to be transformed into one of self-love. The beauty is this in turn creates a life that not only fulfills you and your life's purpose, but also allows everyone touched by your presence to receive this gift.

I look forward to spending this precious time with you.

Welcome to A Woman's Truth.

Sincerely and with love,

Miranda

THE ABUNDANCE OF WEALTH

*True wealth will live on far beyond
this lifetime, as it is infinite and priceless.*

All too often wealth is aligned just with money. Although having a fat bank account does make you financially wealthy, it is but a slice from the pie of life.

In our world, money has become essential to survive. Yet it is important to remember that it is just a tool. You cannot actually eat or build a shelter with money. In fact, in modern times, we have less and less physical contact with the real McCoy. Cash, it seems, is the last stand, as the domain of money becomes more and more aligned with the worlds of technology and illusion.

Even more fascinating is how the exchange of money nowadays is almost entirely built on trust. In reality, all that changes hands are pieces of paper with numbers on them. In and of themselves they are worthless. The piece of paper represents the true value. Moreover, this worth is only realized if people honor and respect the financial agreement represented by the piece of paper. Indeed, collection agencies only exist because these agreements are broken. On every dollar bill, the words 'In God We Trust' are clearly written. Yet, perhaps the words should read 'In each other we trust' to remind us of the exchange to be honored.

Therefore, if money is only one aspect of wealth, even though it is the most coveted, how else are you wealthy in this world? The beauty of *real* wealth is that it is priceless. Meaning it cannot be bought by money and is bountiful in its endless supply. What a concept!

what is the wealth that cannot be lost or stolen?

what is the wealth that will live on as a legacy to who you truly are?

This abundance resides in the realm beyond monetary value. It is what money cannot buy. It lives in the power and riches of love. It is a smile, a hug and an exploration of the Self or a connection to Source. It is the miracle of a dawn and sunset. It is the holding of a newborn baby and the celebration of a life fully lived. It is kindness, consideration, compassion and gratitude.

All of these and more have no financial value or relationship to money, yet they will make you rich beyond your wildest dreams, filling you deep within your being and feeding your soul.

Embracing an abundance of internal wealth encourages the material world of prosperity to be drawn to you like a magnet. The outer world then starts to mirror the inner world and your own personal vision of wealth, riches, prosperity and abundance will be able to reign in all areas of your life.

This golden nugget is the seed of wealth created by the knowledge, wisdom and insight that true fortune is born from the well of your internal being. Couple this with a deep sense of gratitude for all that you have received and a heart-felt appreciation for the riches of love and grace in your life and you will feel wealthy.

"When I bought my home I realized that I was spending large amounts of time pondering how to furnish it. Some areas were simple. It was about placing what I already owned and enjoyed. Other areas needed a new and specific piece of furniture. Especially since, I seem to make the whole house into an altar! After a while, I realized that if I only spent this much energy on furnishing the state of my mind, many areas of my life would change for the better. Even though the three foot jade Quan Yin statue, who is the goddess of compassion, may be out of my price range, I can still refurnish my mind freely by inviting in more compassion towards others and myself. This would be a wonderful replacement for my old beaten up literary of anger and resentment. The beauty is that refurnishing my mind is free and can continually evolve if it is not working. I can change it in an instant. Not quite so easy with a sofa!" ~ Miranda

With the concept that accumulating wealth can begin with a new state of mind, the potent questions to ask are:

◆ *How does having money impact your life?*

◆ *where does the belief that you need money limit your vision?*

Take A Moment To Ponder Your Natural Wealth And Check The Ones In Which You Feel Abundant.

Do you have a wealth of:

- ◊ Gratitude
- ◊ Knowledge
- ◊ Self-Knowledge
- ◊ Wisdom
- ◊ Intelligence
- ◊ Courage
- ◊ Love
- ◊ Faith Reverence
- ◊ Inspiration
- ◊ Passion
- ◊ Communication
- ◊ Experience
- ◊ Joy
- ◊ Laughter

- ◊ Adventure
- ◊ Forgiveness
- ◊ Generosity
- ◊ Peace of Mind
- ◊ Grace
- ◊ Harmony
- ◊ Purity
- ◊ Self-Respect
- ◊ Creativity
- ◊ Purpose
- ◊ Memories
- ◊ Consciousness
- ◊ Playfulness
- ◊ Intimacy

- ◊ Truth
- ◊ Serenity
- ◊ Confidence
- ◊ Radiance
- ◊ Spontaneity
- ◊ Beauty
- ◊ Compassion
- ◊ Patience
- ◊ Tenderness
- ◊ Kindness
- ◊ Opportunity
- ◊ Self-Discipline
- ◊ Insights
- ◊ Intuition

Please feel free to add your own.

From this perspective, can you see how wealthy you already are and that there is an overflow of natural resources all around you? As you pause to receive these gifts, the belief that money is the only answer will become less ingrained, opening up a space to allow wealth into your life in all shapes and sizes and feed you to overflowing.

From this vantage point, an influx of money may become a simple and natural occurrence.

THE ABUNDANCE OF MONEY

"Not what we have but what we enjoy constitutes our abundance."
~ Epicurus

Imagine you were creating the earth and the human race and you needed a sure fire way to monitor human behavior. Just as doctors pour ink into veins to check for a blockage, watching the flow of obstacles that surround your interactions with money can give the same kind of clues into how your life is running.

Visualize a bird's eye view of your journey and choices around money. Remember this relationship began even before birth. Everyone is born into a situation, which was orchestrated, by your ancestors and immediate family. Even before you were old enough to earn your own money, you were already influenced by whether your parents were rich or poor. Many of your beliefs may only be a continuation of an old cycle filtering down through the generations. Were your parents generous or mean? Did they spend or save?

Did they fret and stress over money or was it never an issue? These and many more experiences form a deep imprint even before you pick up your first coin.

Then along with your history comes your own experience. These impressions start to form your own beliefs surrounding money. Specific events all leave a mark, which then influence your emotions and reactions concerning money. Such as:

- Did you get an allowance?
- Were you the poor or the rich kid?
- Were you expected to be responsible for financial situations at an early age?
- Did you have a job growing up?
- Did you dread asking for money when you needed it or did it come easily?
- Did you have a piggybank and save?

"I remember the first time I had to pay my own electricity bill. I went around turning everything off I could possibly find. My poor father, he had been making this simple request for years, but to no avail because it did not seem important as I was not the one paying the bill!" ~ Miranda

Interestingly one of the first contacts a baby has with money is often putting a coin in their mouth and the immediate response of a parent is to tell them to take it out because it is dirty or dangerous. These reactions can give a lasting impression that money is unclean or could kill you and certainly should not to be embraced openly.

PONDER YOUR FIRST MEMORY WITH MONEY
Go back as far as you can recall and see what influence it had on you:

◆ What happened?

◆ How did it feel?

◆ Are you still living your life through the lens of this experience?

◆ Does this perspective help and support you in living an abundant life?

A vital point to remember about money is that it is only energy. Yet it is taken extremely seriously here on this earth plane. No longer is food or shelter bartered for. Instead, money is used to buy whatever you need or want.

As you can see, your ancestral past partnered up with your own personal experiences of money can lead to many of the choices you may be making around your world of finances today. Without clarity and insight into whether these past impressions serve you, an old distorted belief could well be ruling your relationship with money.

Anyone can be great with money.
With money, greatness is not a talent, but an obligation.
The trick is to be great without money and then it will come.
~ Charles David

Remember, energy follows thought, therefore, there is much power in your thinking. These thoughts then create the world in which you live. It is vital to notice how you phrase your ideas or statements around money.

Which kind of words do you choose?

Are they in the positive or the negative?

Take some time to step away from yourself and observe your own conversations. There is much wisdom in this practice and it will yield you an abundance of information on how you view the world and your life in it.

Notice too, the range of voices that live in your head. These are the silent words spoken only to you and are probably just as powerful, if not more so, than the words you speak aloud. There is always an array of conversations going on, often judging what you are witnessing or experiencing. Some of these ideas may be yours, yet many may come from your familial line or your unconscious. Words or phrases you may have heard your mother say a thousand times, or from your own experiences. Unfortunately, this can lead to an emotional and often distorted response derived from your history. Either way, it is vital for you to learn to differentiate which words or beliefs may be serving or hindering you.

Keep in mind, your choices create your future and you in it.

WHICH OF THE FOLLOWING BELIEFS DO YOU LIVE BY?

- ◊ "I never have enough money."
- ◊ "Money terrifies me."
- ◊ "I wish someone would take care of my finances."
- ◊ "I wish someone would support me."
- ◊ "I wish I could find a rich man."
- ◊ "I am poor."
- ◊ "I wish I had more money."
- ◊ "I never get to buy what I want."
- ◊ "Everything is too costly."
- ◊ "I cannot afford that."
- ◊ "I do not earn enough to cover my outgoings."
- ◊ "I cannot hold onto money."
- ◊ "Money slips through my fingers."
- ◊ "I do not have enough money to save."
- ◊ "I do not have enough for retirement."
- ◊ "I buy what I want."
- ◊ "It is okay to spend money I do not have."
- ◊ "I never get to spend money on me."
- ◊ "Money is bad."
- ◊ "Rich people are greedy and unethical."
- ◊ "I will never be rich."
- ◊ "Other people are rich."

- ◊ "I always watch what I spend."
- ◊ "Life is so expensive."
- ◊ "It is a poor economy."
- ◊ "I find everything I need and can afford."
- ◊ "I am wealthy in many different ways."
- ◊ "We are experiencing a shift in the economy."
- ◊ "What I need will come to me."

what are your own personal stories or beliefs?

*"Riches are not from an abundance
of worldly goods, but from a contented mind."
~ Mohammad*

FOR THE LOVE OF MONEY

"The love of money is the root of all evil."
~ Bible

This original quotation from the Bible is often confused and misquoted as 'Money is the root of all evil'. Yet with either quote, money is not the culprit. The one wielding the wealth decides whether it is used for good or bad. It is rather like blaming a kitchen knife or a car for committing a crime. Yes, both can be used as lethal weapons, yet they are meant for chopping food or transportation. It is the person using the knife or behind the wheel who chooses otherwise.

You decide how money is earned, used, spent, borrowed, given or squandered. Just as in all areas of your life, you are the writer, director, orchestrator, producer and protagonist. Money is a tool; it is a representation of your energy or your life in motion. It will follow and amplify the direction you are already moving in.

Whoever you truly were before acquiring any money is the same person that will show up after acquiring any newfound riches. Therefore, it is vital to know if the choices you are making and the direction you are moving in is the right action for you. Otherwise, you may be investing in a well that is already dry or amplifying behaviors, which no longer serve you or others.

Have you ever noticed how, when your survival needs are being challenged, money seems to become the enemy or at least, the lack of it does? Remember, money in and of itself is not the problem. It is much more valuable to look at what belief may be blocking the flow of money or where you are investing your time, money or energy without getting a decent return.

Once you are elevated out of survival, space is then available for the gifts that money can bring. This is basically, freedom of choice. When you are no longer dependent on others financially and you have a surplus of money to play with, life becomes full of choices; whether to work or play, stay home or travel, cook or go out to eat, get support or do it alone.

This freedom of choice is what gives you the space to breathe and to be open to possibility. This really is the ultimate gift of money. It quickly becomes clear why forming a love affair with money's generous and abundant nature is worthwhile. As a human being living in these times, you are intrinsically tethered to its benefits.

Money in this day and age equals freedom of choice.

GRATITUDE IN THE LAND OF PLENTY

Gratitude is the most fertile soil in which to plant the seeds of desire.

Have you ever received such an amazing gift, which was so moving, that it stopped you in your tracks and allowed you to spontaneously bask in the depths of deep gratitude? Often in life, small yet amazing miracles of support, love and grace are raining down continuously, however, it is easy to remain oblivious to their touch and carry on regardless.

In a world where the programming is to yearn for more, to be more, to earn more, to do more and to have more, it is easy to forget to be grateful for all you already have.

There is a lore, which speaks about the idea that to become incarnate as a human being, you need to have experienced ten thousand previous existences, before you are ready to exist here on earth. This might seem like a tall order, yet the philosophy speaks of the gift of a human life being a rare and precious occurrence. Unlike other mammals, humans have the ability to exist in physical form, yet embrace a spiritual life as well. What if you were to see yourself as a rare and unique gift, how would you choose live your life differently? The point of these teachings is for you to own up to whom you truly are and live a life connected to your spiritual heritage. Otherwise, it is as though you are selling yourself as a diamond for the price of day old bread.

How are you living your life?

Do you relish in the beauty of your rare exquisite qualities as a shining gem or are you simply experiencing being chopped spinach?

From this perspective, it is clear how life is a privilege. Therefore, pause and be still long enough to ponder the abundance and plenty, which surrounds you and is always supporting you in this present time.

America truly is a land of plenty, filled with the blessings of clean water, an abundance of food, shelter and the tools readily available to take care of yourself. Couple this with the desire to luxuriate in modern technologies and comforts and it certainly seems there is much for which to be grateful. Yet it is fascinating to notice how many of the new technologies of modern day living can actually end up being harmful if overused. They may well be fast, convenient and stimulating, however, they also have the ability to inhibit your capacity to connect, ground and support yourself, as nature intended.

"As a yoga teacher, I notice how tight people's hips and lower backs are. My sense is that sitting in chairs is a major cause. In countries where squatting on the ground is the normal way to sit, well I doubt they need yoga." ~ Miranda

Therefore, ask yourself how much money is enough?

Take a moment to ponder the expression, **'Waste not, want not'**. As a culture, it seems as though there is a sad evolution that allows squandering and consuming to be a normal part of life. The human race is literally destroying their resources. This wastefulness is the opposite of appreciation and value.

The good news is that there is a growing movement supporting recycling, composting, clean fuel and environmentally safe products. Yet, it is still in its infancy stage. The beauty is that each of you has a responsibility in choosing consciously to clean up your own act; a difference can be made as a whole.

Change begins with each individual.

As the water in your lake is cleansed, purified and vitalized, you become a ripple and an echo that can reach the farthest shore. Be conscious about bringing the act of recycling and composting into your own life. This simply means becoming aware of recycling what you already have as this will increase the opportunity to receive something new.

WAYS TO RECYCLE THE WORLD OF MONEY AND MATERIAL GOODS:

◆ **Go through your house and belongings and give away what you do not need.**
Remember one woman's trash can be another woman's treasure!

◆ **Buy second hand**
Instead of automatically buying brand spanking new, see if you can find a source to support the natural flow of exchange. This becomes a wonderful ebb and flow and there is no waste to deal with.

◆ **Trade and barter**
This ancient method of exchange is slowly coming back into fashion. Instead of using the energy of money, you trade your services or goods for someone else's. As long as everyone is equally valued, the cycle remains complete.

"I sometimes trade a private yoga session for home grown organic vegetables. I have to say, I get much more excited by the basket of vibrant and fresh food, than I do about a piece of paper with numbers and a signature." ~ Miranda

◆ **Recycle**
The act of recycling requires discipline, diligence and mindfulness. Yet, these are the exact qualities, which will benefit your finances and general level of consciousness surrounding the expenditure of your energy.

◆ **Make or grow your own**
There is something quite magical about creating your own product. Yes, to make your own lotion or soap will take time, but it is your energy and love that is breathed into the process. In addition, to receive a homemade gift can be a precious moment.

"I decided that I no longer wanted to water what I cannot eat. Therefore, I dug up the lawn and planted a vegetable garden. To wander out and pick lunch or dinner is a pause in my day and is very different from digging through the refrigerator. In that moment of harvest, I am at the mercy of Mother Nature because I have to follow her pace. Watching the tomatoes slowly turn red is a true act of patience and sharing my lettuces with caterpillars is a forced act of generosity!" ~ Miranda

◆ Giving and receiving

When the channels of generosity and appreciation are open, life can become quite delicious! The secret is to keep this natural ebb and flow of giving and receiving in balance.

You will know when you are giving too much because you will be exhausted and it will not be from having too much fun the night before! If you are demanding too much from others, your conscience will guide you. Although you may feel uncomfortable in this imbalance, often anger or resentment makes you feel justified. Either way a good night's sleep, communicating or some nourishing food or water will set you straight.

"I always know when I have given too much and am depleted, because the action of giving suddenly becomes cold, heartless and another 'have to' and is often fueled with resentment. Yet, when I am in my flow, open to all the love and support that surrounds me, then to give back is as though I also receive a gift." ~ Miranda

Gratitude is like a golden thread that weaves its way throughout your life and imbues all of who you are. Because of its essence, it seems to multiply upon itself and literally increases or intensifies whatever you are already experiencing.

Remember, begin and end your day with appreciation for all that you have. Whenever you feel resistance or resentment, replace it with a sense of gratitude.

This small gesture will help you to reframe the task at hand. When you bring gratitude into the mix, the essential reason why you are doing something becomes apparent. This little shift into gratitude will get the juices flowing and will prepare you to receive.

Next time you sit down to settle your accounts, take a moment before you begin and invoke a sense of gratitude that you have some resources and let this fertile energy support you while paying your bills.

HOW DO YOU PAY YOUR BILLS?

◆ Do you pay them begrudgingly or thankfully?

◆ Do you pay them on time or stressfully leave them to the last minute or until they are past due?

◆ Do you have a specific space to keep your bills where they are organized and stay in your consciousness so they are not forgotten?

◆ Do you have rhythm and a routine to pay your bills on a regular basis?

◆ Do you actually read the bill and notice when you are being over charged?

◆ Do you contact the company to get credit?

◆ Do you check your credit card bills to make sure they are all your charges?

◆ Do you have enough income to cover your outflow?
If you do not, obviously bill paying becomes an action that you will dread and will cause the survival aspect of yourself to freak out!

◆ Even when there is not enough money to cover the bills, do you put your head in the sand and ignore them or do you pay off what you can and keep in communication with your debtor?
This will provide a level of relief and accomplishment, however small.

WRITE DOWN ALL FOR WHICH YOU ARE GRATEFUL:

Gratitude is the open door to abundance.

Allow one idea to lead to another. What will become vividly apparent is that you already live in a world of overwhelming abundance and that you are already truly wealthy.

*"Do not spoil what you have by desiring what you have not.
Remember that what you now have was once
among the things you only hoped for."
~ Epicurus*

THE ILLUSION OF MONEY
The mythical world of finance.

No longer do we barter eggs for cloth or even gold for food. In fact, money has become such an illusion that cash is now seldom used as we wheel and deal in the electronic world of finance. In our world of literal inflation, where money in its original form does not actually exist, it is overspent left, right and center by individuals and governments. Strangely, society actually encourages you to buy objects that you cannot afford and to live beyond your means. Perhaps this is more in alignment with the idea that money is an illusion, yet right now, it is rather like building a house of cards on sand. Eventually it will collapse, even if more money that is illusionary is pumped in. Sooner or later, it will fall.

"Up until a few years ago I had never had any debt. I was proud of this fact and always figured ways to pay upfront. I rented my homes and never owned a new car! Yet, when I started to inquire deeper into my belief around debt, I realized it was fear based; that I would be tied down, owned, literally indebted. Then all of a sudden, many outlandish opportunities were laid out in front of me and I am now the illusionary owner of a house and two cars. No, I do not own them outright, and yes, they all enhance my life. Ultimately, it was about walking head-first into the world of debt with all my fears screaming at me and realizing that not only can I survive in debt, I can actually thrive if the debts are chosen wisely." ~ Miranda

The important part to remember is that there is still plenty of money to go around. Once you are in alignment with an abundant flow, this will become apparent.

Imagine that you were in a river always flowing, and then somehow you were lost and ended up in the desert; parched, poor and thirsty. The choice to be made is to return to the abundant river. This means looking at past actions and decisions that may have diverted you off track in the first place.

UNVEIL YOUR MONEY RELATIONSHIP

Inquiry reveals all.

It is vital for your own personal relationship with money to be brought into the open. Then you will clearly see all your strengths and weaknesses. From this vantage point, new actions, choices and decisions can be made.

CONTEMPLATE THESE QUESTIONS:

◆ How do you feel when you have enough money in the bank?

◆ How do you feel when you do not have enough to cover the basics?

◆ Do you save money?

◇ Yes   ◇ No

◆ How do you feel when you have savings?

◈ Are you in debt?

   ◊ Yes   ◊ No

◈ Do you know how much you owe?

◈ How do you feel when you are in debt?

◈ Do you lend money?

   ◊ Yes   ◊ No

◈ How do you feel when you lend money?

◆ How do you feel when you owe money?

◆ How do you feel when you renege on paying off money?

◆ How do you feel when someone does not pay you the money you are owed?

◆ How does it feel when you are ripped off?

◆ How do you feel when you get a bargain?

◈ Do you pay your bills on time?

　　◊ Yes　　◊ No

◈ What else causes you stress around money?

◈ By receiving a huge influx of money, how would your life change?

Do not sacrifice your health for money.

THE BONDAGE OF MONEY

*If the truth shall set us free,
can we say the same for money?*

Have you ever asked yourself why you actually want more money? For many, knowing that there is money in the bank eases feelings of fear and gives a sense of security. Yet, often it is not so much about having the actual money, but more about what it can or will provide for you.

There was an old beggar.

All his life he sat on an old chest begging for what he needed to survive.

The villagers took care of him knowing he was one of them.

As he reached old age, he died.

Peacefully hunched over on his chest with his eyes closed, his breath stopped.

The villagers gathered together and picked up his body to organize a burial for him.

As they went to pick up the chest, they could hardly lift it, for its heavy weight.

When they opened it up, it was full to the brim with gold coins.

To their astonishment,

They realized this beggar had been richer than the whole village put together.

Are you sitting on a pot of gold and not utilizing it?

Are you hoarding money just for the sake of having more?

Remember, Money Is Just A Tool.

Through scarcity and lack, it can bind you to relationships, situations and fears. Yet, through choosing to live in abundance and mindfully managing your finances, you can be the benefactor of great freedom and possibilities. Having money for money's sake is limiting. Yet, when you have money as an expression of who you are and you allow its gifts and presence to provide for you, it will set you free.

It is fascinating that something so intangible has so much power.

Pause a moment to see where your relationship with money is controlling your life. How you invest your money and what kind of return you are making can be used as a very powerful indication as to how you are spending your time and energy.

If you feel as though you are working too hard and getting very little in return, it may be time to change your direction. Obviously there are situations, such as building a new business where there is a need to invest in the creation. This is appropriate for a period of time, yet, if after a few years, you are still not receiving any profit, there is something amiss. This can be translated into many areas of life. Overly investing into a relationship or a charitable project can be as harmful as investing in a bad deal. It is vital to question the investment versus the return.

*Are you being fairly refunded
for the amount of energy you are expending in your life?*

Obviously, this does not always have to boil down to money. The exchange could be a trade, a gift or an act of service. The point is to discern whether the exchange is in balance. If there is equilibrium, there is no room for resentment or anger to buildup.

"I have noticed that as I get older, I can no longer get away with not doing what I came here to do. It seems as though in my twenties and even my thirties, I could dabble in all sorts of career moves; some less appealing than others. Yet, today in my forties, it seems as though to get the return I desire, I have to be aligned with my purpose here on earth and using the gifts and talents, I was born and blessed with. This certainly feels like a good exchange." ~ Miranda

MONEY AND SELF WORTH

Money is a vital part of the world.

Money has the ability to represent health, strength, honor, generosity, trust and beauty as conspicuously as the want of it can represent illness, weakness, greed, disgrace, meanness and ugliness. It is directly connected to your sense of self worth. Is having money what gives you confidence? Or is it the belief that you deserve an abundantly good life that attracts prosperity?

As you know, your thoughts attract energy. The good news is that money *is* energy. Therefore, if you believe you are rich and prosperous on a conscious and unconscious level, then the chances are that you will be affluent. It really is that simple. This is why it is imperative to look at all the old subconscious belief patterns that are formed through family, society, gender and experience. If there is a deep driving belief that you will never be rich, then unfortunately this can become your reality.

Therefore, as money is energy it is essential to have a clear intention in order to manifest its gifts. Make sure your longing for money directly contributes to the quality of your life and others. Be conscious that the desire or need is not rooted in fear, lust or greed as this would not be aligned with your truth or integrity. Unfortunately, a fear-based need for money, can powerfully influence the method taken to produce the desired income. How you experience the course of action taken is just as important as the result. If you are miserable in how you are making your money, it is time to ask the question; is the money worth the agony?

The gift in this scenario is its ability to inspire change and to choose a way of earning money that aligns with your authentic sense of self. Also, remember prosperity and abundance are not only about money.

To have an abundance of love in your life can be a much richer experience than having a huge wad of cash. An overflow of support, comfort, joy and time can also make you rich beyond your wildest dreams.

TAKE A MOMENT TO NOTICE AND CIRCLE THE AREAS OF YOUR LIFE THAT ARE THE POOREST:

- Money
- Health
- Love
- Time
- Relationships
- Play
- Partnership
- Honesty
- Intimacy
- Adventure
- Sex
- Friendships
- Creativity
- Shelter
- Food

- Nature
- Support
- Rest
- Comfort
- Self-Esteem
- Style
- Happiness
- Joy
- Confidence
- Exercise
- Forgiveness
- Faith
- Family
- Inspiration
- Savings

- Investments
- Retirement
- Dreams
- Communication
- Fun
- Laughter
- Culture
- Sleep
- Compassion
- Beauty
- Sensuality
- Passion
- Security
- Other

*wherever there is a deficit, pay attention
and make new choices, which will fill the void.*
~ Miranda

MONEY AND EMOTIONS

Calamity in your life is a sure sign to pay attention.

Have you ever noticed periods in your life where chaos seems to reign? Your car breaks down, your computer does not work, and you drop your favorite cup.

Part of the upset around these dramas is that repairing them takes time and money. Often, when there are consecutive mishaps, it is a sign that you may be out of balance. This could be emotionally, mentally, physically or spiritually. Money issues can clearly reflect your internal state of affairs.

When misfortune befalls, pay attention and inquire internally as to what is pulling you off center. If money is pouring out of your life in an uncontrolled manner, so is your energy. Therefore, it is time to plug up the holes. If your money feels as though it is in chaos or spinning out of control, it is a symbol that your thoughts may be doing the same. Just as you are encouraged to listen to the symbolism of your body, money or lack thereof can also be one of your toughest guides, yet most impactful teachers.

When it comes to investing your money, emotions can often undermine the success of your choices. Unfortunately, investing is not a natural process for most people. It requires patience and often goes against the grain of some basic human tendencies. The best investors seem to have great control over their emotions.

It has been said that sociopaths make good investors!

The point is that when you are overly emotional or out of balance, you can become reactive and many a bad decision can be made. This could be as simple as spending the rent money on a pair of shoes or choosing to eat a tub of ice cream for dinner.

"I have a deep attachment to my money plants. They live in the money corners of my home and I tend to them often. A while ago, all my plants started to die. Leaves fell off or went brown and little flies were nesting in the soil. A number of people told me, I was overwatering them.

Yet, I have a strange propensity to think you cannot overdo water, whether you are a plant or a body! Nevertheless, as I watched my beloved plants shrivel and die, I became extremely nervous as I treat them as symbols of my relationship with money. So, I stopped watering them. The dry barren soil made me nervous, yet my plants began to thrive and there was new growth and they became green again. It was not until later that I understood the real lesson. Water depicts emotions. Therefore, it seems as though I was being overly emotional around my relationship with money, just as I was over watering my plants." ~ Miranda

THE BOND OF MONEY AND FEAR

We are only as strong as our weakest link.

The following exercise can be a powerful and life changing experience. Often decisions in life are made out of fear and limitation. As you become aware of any old, outdated beliefs, you can then question these perspectives and decide whether they are actually aligned with your current truth.

Money can also be brandished as a weapon when it is used as a form of control. Often the desire to have power over another originates from a fear or insecurity. If you feel that you are instilling control by using money in an area of your life, pay attention. On the other hand, maybe there is someone controlling you through the dominance and power of their money. Either way, this is an area to clean up and bring the balance of partnership back into play.

Money can be wielded like a sword of light or a machete of fear. As a warrior in the world, how do you choose to use money? Do you use it as a weapon or a chalice?

As you inquire into these old perceptions and they are brought to light, you can then choose a new awareness and replace them with a different and more empowering mindset. This allows your psyche to be open to receive the always available abundance. When you are instilled with fear, it is similar to a kink in the hose or gripping too tightly. The ability to receive prosperity is limited and reduced.

Faith and fear cannot exist in the same breath.
Which one do you choose for yourself?

One choice is to believe you are weak and unable to take care of yourself. Another is to believe in your strength, courage and resourcefulness. When you remember who you are without letting fear eclipse your true essence, you are conquering fear and you are living with the fundamental faith of who you are.

ANSWER THE FOLLOWING FOR MORE AWARNESS:

◆ **What is your deepest fear surrounding money?**
It will possibly feel disempowering, belittling or uncomfortable to say.

◆ **How does this belief support you?**
This belief has aligned itself with an old wound. It will not be rational. As strange as it sounds, the psyche forms beliefs for a reason. Therefore, no matter how crazy the belief may sound in the cold light of day, on some level it has been serving you. It will usually be connected to your survival. To answer this question you will need to think outside of the box and ignore the voice in your head that tells you that this fear does not serve you.

◆ **When did you form this belief?**
It is important to get a sense of when it began. Do not think too hard, just allow whatever image or thoughts arise or go with your first hit.

◆ **Deeply thank this belief for trying to save you.**
   This belief has probably been there a long time and was formed out of survival to keep you safe. Even if the belief is distorted and maybe a little crazy, still thank it. Our wounds are never sane!

◆ **What is a new belief that supports, loves and nourishes all of who you are?**
   This belief will have the energy of abundance, freedom, power, expansion and a deep-seated belief in your own ability and brilliance. This is something you would wish for one you dearly love.

◆ **Clearly, write out this belief.**
   Keep teasing the new conviction until it becomes a single sentence. There is no need for a story at this point. The clearer and simpler the statement, the easier it will be to repeat in your life. Examples would be 'I gratefully receive abundance and prosperity in my life.' 'It is safe to thrive and succeed in all areas of my life.' 'I am thriving and successful in all areas of my life.'

◆ **Repeat this belief to yourself many, many, many times a day.**
   Say it while falling asleep, upon waking, while standing in line, while exercising or while meditating.

◆ **To get two birds with one stone, do your Kegel exercises at the same time.**
   This will contain and draw in your energies and help strengthen your resolve.

Looking at old limiting beliefs is hard work and can be uncomfortable. Be loving and kind with yourself and allow all emotions to arise. Often, with loaded topics such as money and sex, many suppressed feelings have been stored. These inquiries shed a light on the beliefs within your cellular memory. The result is a fantastic clarity and lightness, as you are no longer burdened by the weight of an old pattern, habit or belief that was deeply rooted in your past. This process takes courage, yet it is this fortitude that will form a loving, committed and respectful relationship with money.

As you go through life, old patterns around money may arise. You can carry out the same process with each one until you are a clean slate with many new systems that will bring all your heart's desires.

Fear makes the wolf bigger than he is.
~ German Proverb

YOUR PARTNERSHIP WITH MONEY
Is it a love affair or heading for a divorce?

Money is actually one of the most potent, primary and in-your-face relationships you can have. A day does not go by without you at some point thinking, using, talking about or earning some money. Yet strangely enough, money is a topic many people do not even want to discuss. Talking about money does not mean you have to hang your dirty laundry around debt or bad spending. This is more about getting complete clarity regarding how much money is actually being spent on a daily basis.

As you know, being unconscious of an impending situation such as not having enough money can easily lead to fear, panic and a sense of powerlessness. Just as in any relationship, if there is no communication or honesty, it is very hard for the partnership to thrive and prosper.

This journey ahead is about you facing your relationship with money full on. Become honest with yourself and your spending habits. Part of our internal work will be to write down everything you are spending by using A Revealing Money Chart on page 85. You can download copies from Miranda's website at:

www.MirandaJBarrett.com/resources/the-abundance-of-wealth.

THE MONEY CHART WILL HELP GUIDE YOU IN:

◊   Prioritizing what is most important, therefore decreasing your stress levels.

◊   Spending your money wisely.

◊   Letting money become your friend and ally and making decisions that will allow money to work for you.

◊   Permitting this weighted currency to give you the freedom it can afford.

For some of you this may ignite a feeling of deep dread, especially if you know your money is out of balance and you do not want to know by how much. Becoming clear and more decisive about your money situation could possibly result in you no longer using shopping as therapy and as a way to numb some unwelcome emotions. As you move through the teachings of 'A Woman's Truth' you will gain courage and the knowledge that you can face whatever emotion comes your way, however large the grievance. Therefore, these potent addictive tools of spending, eating or electronics will no longer be needed as a survival mechanism. The result is you will receive as much pleasure in saving money as you do from spending it.

"A cat bitten once by a snake dreads even rope."
~ Arab proverb

A TRICK TO MONEY IS HAVING SOME

Is life just one big oversized game of Monopoly?

Everyone is playing the game of money. The good news is if you understand that money is a pawn in this adventure and that you are a player, then at least you can attempt to not take it quite so seriously and at the same time, honor the rules and play to win.

One of the most poignant laws of the game of life is that in this day and age, some money is needed to exist. Therefore, if you do not have enough, it is easy to fall back into fear and survival mode. This is prompted by the belief that a lack of money will lead to the inability to put food in your belly or a roof over your head. Life in this vein is beyond stressful because you are facing the possibility of extinction and every part of your physical body is wired to keep the species alive. Therefore, it is obvious that triggering your survival instinct is not an optimal position.

If you are in debt and have limited financial resources, know it is time to turn the ship around. Because you are the captain and director of your life, you are the only one who can accomplish a change of direction. As you are now learning some new rules, you will have all the tools necessary to take responsibility and become accountable, and start to live in security rather than scarcity. Your relationship with money is no different to your connection with your body.

"I see this again and again as a nutritional consultant. People come to me with an ailment. The changes are made for a short while and they feel better. Yet, over time, the old habits of refined sugar or not drinking enough water creep back in and they wonder why their energy drops and the symptoms re-appear." ~ Miranda

Imagine being highly in debt and inheriting a million dollars. For a while, you are out of survival mode and probably thoroughly enjoying yourself. Yet if you do not change the habits and patterns surrounding your behavior with money that got you into debt in the first place, in time you will have squandered your inheritance and be back in debt, right where you started.

For the outcome to be different, the terrain needs to change.

"One of my teachers told me years ago that in order to be spiritual in the West, you first need to be prosperous. I took this to heart and I spend many of my waking hours being mindful and diligent to bring in enough money to be able to cover my basics, because I would have the space, shelter and luxury to meditate. However, just to be clear, the tables do turn sometimes. There has been many an instance when, in desperation, I have sat and prayed for clarity and guidance around a financial situation and how to bring in more money. In this case I am first being spiritual in order to be prosperous." ~ Miranda

In this game called life, it is imperative that your higher Self chooses the rules and makes sure that the other aspects of your being are playing along and behaving. When you either go on a shopping spree, in person or online, know that this could be a part of you rebelling because it feels ignored and under-nourished. It is a sign that you may be out of balance. If this is a habitual pattern, it is vital to find out what the 'shopper' in you really needs. She may be jeopardizing your safety and security by potentially putting you in the red.

Staying afloat while in debt takes a tremendous amount of energy.

The other point to remember is everyone will spend money on what they deem as important or of value. This is the same with time.

"I have noticed that sometimes I have a list of vital tasks to accomplish and I am on a collision course with stress to get them done and then the 'love of my life' or my daughter calls. Suddenly the 'to do' list seems to vanish into thin air as my desire to connect with this person overrides all else." ~ Miranda

Part of the game is about deciding what is important to you and making sure you have enough money to comfortably afford these essentials. Financial security needs to become a high priority on the list, therefore allowing the survival aspect of the self to calm down and not drag you from your balanced center out of fear.

Some people love the thrill of playing on the edge of financial wisdom and thrive on taking risks with money. Even if this is your excitement of choice, having a nest egg is always vital for security reasons. It is imperative to know who is making the rules. If this incessant risk taking is being fired-up and fueled by the need for adrenaline to get you through your day or out of a deep-seated self-loathing, then these emotional reactions need to be addressed.

Most people do find a sense of peace and well-being from having a substantial bank account balance and some savings tucked away. Humans are no different to squirrels in how they hoard their nuts for the winter. This instinct is designed for longevity.

Ultimately, this world of money is your game.
You get to decide how you want to play.
Decide to win.

IN WHAT DO YOU INVEST?

While chasing after money you will never have enough. Yet, when your life is on purpose and filled with gratitude, then there is prosperity. Stop wanting and start receiving.

The definition of investment is: "To furnish with power and authority in order to gain a profit". Therefore, by its very nature, successful investing demands for you to be balanced and in your center. Oddly, the word investment is usually found on the pages of The Wall Street Journal or lives in the vocabulary of people with an abundance of money. Yet in reality, everyone in life is making investments daily, with their time, money and energy. Remaining conscious of these investments will yield you important and significant clues about how you choose to live your life and the priorities you set for yourself.

A wise investor is someone who looks for long-term opportunities and is patient in their approach. They are often open to seeing what else they could invest in; they do not risk everything on one endeavor. There is also a train of thought in the investment world that it is better to invest against the crowd, avoiding the hype and staying in your own sphere of what is the right action for your own prosperity.

If you translate this into to the world of investing heavily in yourself, you will see that to become your own proficient and worldly-wise investor rewards you an enormous profit. This return could be in the realm of money, energy, health and happiness.

IMAGINE SAVING MONEY IN A PIGGY BANK:

◆ In whom are you investing?

◆ Does the piggy bank have your name on it or someone else's?

Be honest with yourself.

*If you are not the person you are investing in,
it is time to make some changes!*

There are times when other people or ventures are important, yet it is vital to always fill your own well first. From this overflow, there will be plenty to invest in others without it having any detrimental effect on your well-being. Experiment substituting the word 'buy' with 'invest' in your daily vocabulary.

*Never give from the depths of your well,
always give from your overflow.*
~ Rumi

Rather than asking the question 'Shall I buy this?' instead ask:

Shall I invest in this?

It gives money spending a completely new dimension. In addition, you could ask:

Shall I invest my time in this?

The following is another tool to gain control of all your expenditures and thus your life:

Is this a good investment of my energies?

NOTHING IS FOR FREE
Pay attention to the price you pay.

Everything in life is an exchange of energy, whether it is time or money. It has been said the most precious commodity is time, because it is the one thing in this human plane that cannot be recaptured. You may have noticed that when something is offered free of charge, there is often a condition. Perhaps it is a purchase made to get the free offer or it takes time to get the deal. In life, there is always an exchange:

Money for time ~ Time for money ~ Energy for money
Money for energy ~ Time for energy ~ Energy for time

As you navigate through your life, periodically pause for a moment to become conscious if the exchanges that are happening feel like a fair trade and are ones you want to be a part of. Remember, by saying no to a request or a demand that is not your truth is highly empowering and honest. If you find you are relinquishing your power by saying yes when you mean no, the exchange will not only cost you your hard-earned money or time, but also your integrity.

"My father instilled in me a very strong work ethic. The front of the hand is that I am not afraid to work hard, be responsible and show up. Yet the back of the hand is that I can have a tendency to work too much and not play enough. Obviously, my child aspect has an issue with this!" ~ Miranda

EXPLORE YOUR RELATIONSHIP OF WORK AND PLAY:

◆ How is your work ethic?

◆ Is your work ethic in balance with your world of play?

There is always a balance between the energy that needs to be spent in order to get a return and being open to receiving miracles. Yet if your alignment is that someone or something else will take care of you, this can leave you in a position of weakness and dependency. This belief does not encourage you to create a life where you are doing what you love and receiving a reward and exchange for your energy and time.

Money is actually a wonderful motivator in life. Think about all the extraordinary businesses and products available, which were born from someone following their inspiration and talent and being motivated by a need to provide for themselves or their families.

"I have known a number of trust fund babies in my life. Beautiful and extraordinary beings, yet without the motivating factor of having to make money each day, they seemed lost and unable to gather their will or life forces to fully create their lives."
~ Miranda

Look back over your life and see how money has been your teacher. How your desire or need for this medium of exchange has propelled you forward even when you may have wanted to choose inertia or stay in bed!

Be grateful to its teachings and inspiration and that this survival instinct is alive and kicking in you. The desire for money often ignites the will and life force needed to support the longing to thrive and succeed. Know that you have the ability and power to provide and take care of yourself. With this knowledge, you are set free.

"My personal belief is that we do not actually leave home until we are completely financially independent. The day that we are no longer reliant on someone else, is the day we can truly claim our own power. It seems we only need to experience this fully once in a lifetime to remember we are strong, capable and resourceful. Even if situations change and we do become reliant on someone again, it may be a choice to be vulnerable, yet deep down knowing there is always the ability to be self-sufficient." ~ Miranda

GIVING

In giving, we also receive.

The concept of tithing and charity has been around for hundreds of years. In its simplest sense, it is the practice of bestowing a portion of your income to an individual, an institution or a situation. This gesture can allow for a greater return of your personal income, as you align with the ebb and flow of giving and receiving.

THE QUESTIONS TO ASK HERE ARE:

◆ Are you a natural philanthropist?
   Do you have an inclination to increase the well-being of humankind?

◆ Do you feel you connect and live in the abundance of the universe?

◆ Do you give freely?

◆ Do you over give and have little left for yourself?

◆ Do you give when you do not really want to?

◆ Do you say yes when you mean no?

◆ Do you give with resentment or generosity in your heart?

◆ Why do you give?

◆ Does the gesture of giving come from your head or your heart?

In many traditions, it is encouraged to give ten percent of your earnings away. This keeps the channels of the inflow and the outflow open and encourages more life abundance.

"Feed your faith and your fears will starve to death"
~ Author Unknown

GIVING UP

As we release the old and the tired, a space is crafted for new beginnings and endless possibilities.

During this time together, as your journey and life are aligning with who you truly are, there is an opening for you to empower yourself and consciously choose what you want. The more awareness you have around what is benefiting or hindering you, the more you can take deliberate control of what is the right action. This will reign in your energies, your power and your light, embodying you with a life force and magnitude that will fuel your heart's desire.

The question to ask here is:

Do you have an area in your life that is out of control?

This will translate into aspects of your world where you are unconsciously spending or draining your time, your money or your energy. It could be a habit that is detrimental to your health and well-being or it could be a pattern of behavior that exhausts you. Choosing to give up and surrender what is no longer productive or beneficial for you, will then allow a new behavior, thought or pattern to be explored.

POSSIBLE HABITS TO GIVE UP:

- ◊ Sugar
- ◊ Caffeine
- ◊ Alcohol
- ◊ Smoking
- ◊ Certain Relationships
- ◊ Spending Habits
- ◊ Splurging
- ◊ Impulse Spending
- ◊ Buying
- ◊ Chocolate
- ◊ Overeating
- ◊ Sodas
- ◊ Saying Yes, But Mean No
- ◊ Comfort Eating
- ◊ Dieting
- ◊ Dependencies
- ◊ Addictions
- ◊ Talking
- ◊ Over-Exercising
- ◊ Overcommitting
- ◊ Overbooking
- ◊ Staying Up Too Late
- ◊ Too Much Media
- ◊ Your Own Personal Sin

◆ **Which of the above would empower you by choosing to refrain from it?**
By taking control, you will be proving to yourself that in reality you are more powerful than a harmful action or an unhealthy belief.

◆ What will you gain by refraining from indulging in these behaviors?

◆ How will you choose to spend this extra energy, time or money?

You are the Captain of your ship, the Queen of your kingdom and the Mistress of your domain. By cleaning out the old and claiming the new, you will allow the bountiful qualities of grace, power and love to rule your world.

INCOME VERSUS OUTCOME

"Annual Income: twenty pounds;
Annual Expenditure: nineteen pounds,
nineteen shillings, six pence.
Result: Happiness.
Annual Income: twenty pounds;
Annual Expenditure: twenty pounds and six pence.
Result: Misery."
~ Quote

In a world where money has become the primary medium for exchange, it is vital to remember that by investing in yourself, you can be abundantly rich and fulfilled. With this in mind, the quality and quantity of your **in**come has a direct correlation to the **out**come. If the income is meager and weak, the outcome will be meager and weak as well. You cannot expect a huge, blazing fire with a couple of damp twigs. Use this analogy in your life to see where your inflow is not supporting your outflow. As this quote suggests, it is all about being conscious and choosing actions, which will result in an outcome of happiness, not misery.

THE QUESTIONS HERE ARE VERY SIMPLE:

◆ Do you know how much money you spend on a weekly or monthly basis?

◆ Does the money that you earn or receive cover these outgoings?

If the answers to either of these questions is no, it is time to look at your money situation. To actually make a list of your monthly outgoings is an empowering act. It places you in the role of a responsible adult making informed decisions regarding your finances and future. There is a huge difference in knowing you have enough money to cover your basic survival needs, verses desperately hoping the check does not bounce or that you still have room left on your credit card. The latter leaves you in a position of fear and stress, which takes its toll on your mind, emotions and body.

SPEND SOME WELL EARNED TIME FILLNG OUT THE REVEALING MONEY CHART:

This will empower and possibly distress you. Yet, knowing where you actually stand financially is far more effective than closing your eyes, crossing your fingers and desperately hoping for the best. Please go to page 85 to fill out the chart or go to www.MirandaJBarrett.com/resources/the-abundance-of-wealth to print out more copies for yourself.

◆ **You will have answers to some of the questions on the chart straight away.**
An example of this is your mortgage or rent.

◆ **You can look up less regular expenses in your checkbook or on your credit card statements.**
Such as a doctor appointments or car repairs.

◆ **Notice where you are spending cash.**
Account for that as well.

◆ **Ask for and keep all receipts.**
It is vital to know every expense even if it is small. Over time, they add up.

◆ **Write out even the smallest expense.**
This includes a bottle of water, a magazine or a tip to a restaurant. You want to be accountable for every morsel so you can see exactly where your money is flowing out.

◆ **One way to keep track is to carry the chart with you and write down whenever you spend any money during a full month.**
In this way, you will cover all of what you are spending.

◆ **It is important to keep track of your credit card expenditures as well.**
That way, you will not have any surprises when the bill comes.

◆ **Keep your finances organized.**
Have files for your receipts, bills and taxes. This will make your dealings with money much clearer. This also sends a message to the universe that you are responsible and have a clear goals and objectives around money.

◆ **Remember stress and anxiety around money is an energy leak.**
Therefore, you are impacted twice. Firstly by not having enough money and secondly by the worry you are experiencing. The best healing is to reorganize your finances in a way that is reassuring to you and aligns with the reality of how much money you actually have.

If you spend less than you make, you will always be rich.

SAVING MONEY
The pot of gold at the end of your rainbow.

Saving money is obviously a good idea. You are your own most important asset. When you save, you are investing in you. This is a clear and outright message to the world that you believe in your own importance, your own worth and your own future. This simple action powerfully unravels the fear of survival and you always have a safety net that will catch you if you have a financial fall from grace. Saving is one of the ultimate declarations of self-love. Yet, as with all aspects of money, there are some basic rules to live by:

◆ **Begin saving today no matter what.**
 Let go of the idea that you have to have a certain amount of money to save. Even if you only save five dollars a month, over years with time being the highest benefactor of investing, even this small amount will add up.

◆ **Give the savings account a title and set a positive intention for the money.**
 Money is energy and energy follows your thoughts, therefore saved money may well eventually end up needing to be used for what you had originally planned. Do not let fear be the motivating factor when you save. Allow thriving adventure and freedom to be your inspiration.

◆ **Make the intention for your savings a proactive one.**
 Examples are a vacation or a down payment to buy a house. The money will flow to whatever you claim. Thus, 'emergency' or 'if I lose my job' money may result in this happening.

- ◈ **Saving money for money's sake will impede the flow.**
  Keep the energy of money moving. Do not sit on your saved money for too long. Money is energy and needs to move. Once you have your desired amount, use it for the intended result.

- ◈ **Changing the place where the money is kept will move the energy.**
  Examples are a new account, bank or hiding place.

- ◈ **Replace old wads of cash with new ones.**
  If you have had a thousand dollars stashed under your mattress, save another thousand and spend the old one. This gives the money back its flow.

- ◈ **Similarly, when a bill comes in, pay it.**
  Letting go of money in an easy and responsible manner keeps you in the flow. Always be in a feeling of gratitude that you have the money as you pay bills. You might be surprised at how quickly the expenditure replaces itself.

- ◈ **Save different amounts in different places.**
  Do not keep all your eggs in one basket. Be creative with money. Save some money in CD's, savings accounts, safe deposit box, cash, currencies, precious metals or gems, such as gold, silver or diamonds.

- ◈ **Do not over save.**
  Money is there to give you the freedom to live your life fully and to explore being creative. Having loads of money hidden away and never using it out of fear is not living. Hoarding money just for the sake of it is a waste of precious time here on earth.

◆ **Always make sure you have what you need to take care of yourself and your dependents or responsibilities.**
This is the first priority.

◆ **Avoid saving schemes that you do not understand or sound too good to be true.**
Get rich quick schemes rarely pay off. The investment industry is full of people trying to profit from others naivety.

◆ **Save for your retirement.**
This type of savings requires a very conservative, consistent, long term and patient approach. The beauty of long-term savings is that when the market is on a rollercoaster ride you are not at its mercy. You can sit tight, breath and know that in another few years it will have leveled out again.

◆ **It is always good to have a few saving projects happening at once.**
Some will be long term such as retirement or a down payment. Others will be more short term, such as a vacation. In addition, there is always that Italian leather bag that is more immediate!

what does saving money mean to you?

ALWAYS ASK YOURSELF:

In what are you choosing to invest?

For some people, saving is actually putting money away in an account and not spending it. Yet for others, it is saving for an item on sale that they may not need.

Remember, when you are obsessed with sales, you are actually investing in the thrill of getting a bargain. You may possibly be buying objects that you do not even need or use, although it will fulfill the lure of getting a good deal. Discern what value the purchase will have in your life and ponder if paying off a debt or saving for a vacation would empower you more.

RETIREMENT IN THE GOLDEN YEARS
Invest in yourself.

Whoever coined the term, 'The Golden Years' was probably someone who had saved plenty of cash to thoroughly enjoy this stage of their life. Yet, if you suddenly had to live on a third of your income when you retire, the shininess of the golden years may well tarnish into the reality of a bleak and meager existence. Therefore, it seems vital that whatever your age and hopefully while you are still young enough to use time to your advantage, that you choose to put money away on a regular basis. This is surely an act of self-love, self-worth and self-respect and paving the way for many glorious and relaxing golden years ahead.

The statistics show that the younger you start saving for retirement the better the financial outcome will be. Even if it is a tiny amount every month, by the time you reach an age where you no longer want to work, the funds you need will have grown and will be available.

"It is the strangest phenomenon. When I finally listened to all the financial advice I had heard over the years and began an automatic transfer out of my checking account into a retirement fund every month, a miracle occurred. I had always believed I could not afford to do this. It seemed that every month the income and outgoing ratio was just too tight. I accepted the illusion there was not enough of a window so I did not set up the transfer of funds and every year my retirement account remained a big fat zero. Then one year I decided to bite the bullet. It is strange how reaching a certain age will force your hand. I took a leap of faith and decided to set up the account anyway. Sometimes the money is still tight, yet strangely not much different from before and the miracle is that I now have a retirement fund to my name. It seems this relocation of funds is working and the advice to save before you spend seems to be paying off." ~ Miranda

The difference between thinking you should save for retirement and actually taking the course of action to set up an account is the difference between getting ready to leap into a swimming pool and never learning to swim. Imagine you are about to take the plunge yet you do not actually know if you will survive. Getting older and becoming less able to work and not having money put aside for these precious years is highly stressful on the survival aspect of your psyche.

It is fine to live in the present moment, yet the survival part of your DNA needs reassurance that your future existence is taken care of. If you are a parent, it is about choosing not to burden your children or other family members. As you experience 'A Woman's Truth' and you claim your power, you will learn that being financially independent, stable and capable of sustaining the lifestyle that you desire is the ultimate strength and freedom. Unfortunately, our innate survival aspect of the brain will not release stress unless it is reassured there are life-sustaining mechanisms in place. This tension lives at a deep unconscious level of not knowing if your future is taken care of, which can slowly chip away at any peace, happiness and security.

Having enough money is the best way to release fears grasp of living in this material world. Therefore, every time you save for yourself, know that the fearful aspect of your survival can calm down and relax. Most of us are familiar with the feeling of not having enough to go around and the crippling panic this invokes. Imagine never having to suffer such anguish again.

As someone so wisely said, "I do not want to outlive my assets." For many, the deepest fear is at the end of their life they will no longer have any control over where or how they live. Yet there is certainly a balance between over saving for the possibility of this daunting outcome and being responsible and mindful of what in reality you may need for your future. Sometimes there can be a tendency to live your life without fullness while you are healthy and able, out of fear of a future involving sickness and dependency.

A vital question to ask is, how much is enough? Fear will never think there is enough for its worst-case scenario. Yet it would be unfortunate to die with mounds of money because you are afraid to follow your heart's desires, your bucket list and live a life of adventure while you still can.

Envision building such an empire, that through the act of conscious choice you allow yourself to feel an emotion rather than defaulting to shopping as therapy. You would save for yourself and your retirement and choose not to live in debt. You would be assured of your survival, deeply relaxing into all the gifts, bounty and possibilities these choices will incur.

Be courageous and invest in yourself. Build savings rather than debt. Change the story and receive as much pleasure from saving as you do from spending.

Remember, one is you giving yourself away. The other is you receiving. By choosing to live in your feminine essence, you will be more open to receiving. Be your own financial advisor and investor. Adorn yourself with security rather than jewelry. Live in the reality of honoring and taking care of yourself and know your future is safer and more secure through this act of self-love.

Choose to cherish yourself enough to secure you financial freedom. Your future far outweighs the thrill of another pair of shoes or a handbag! Choose to invest in yourself. Choose to be wise.

Next time you enjoy sitting under the shade of a tree, remember it was planted many years before. Therefore, it is with investing time as your most precious commodity, will you allow the seeds of your investment to grow eventually into your shelter from life's storms.

THE BIGGEST GIFT OF DEATH

Bequeath your loved ones a priceless endowment.
Give them the precious and much needed space to grieve
and mourn, rather than worry about the finances
and arrangements of your funeral and belongings.

Imagine when you die being able to leave your estate in such grand order that your loved ones had the space, time, money and support to fully grieve, to fall apart and to be conscious of their heart felt loss for you. The other scenario is when you die, your dearly beloved family, partner or friends are left with debt, a huge mess to clear up, the confusion of not knowing your wishes and a deep sense of overwhelm as they try to navigate their grief with a brand new horrendous full time job of sorting out your death after life.

Although it might seem mercenary to leave your loved ones with resources and an organized and updated will or living trust, it truly is the biggest gift you can give. This scenario allows for your wishes to be fulfilled and for the culmination of shock, disbelief and even anger to be felt and leaned into by those mourning you.

When you organize and prepare your death, there is space for the gamut of overwhelming emotions that grief weaves through those left mourning. In reality, there is no skipping grief. Yes, you can numb, drug or eat your way through it, yet eventually grief still seems to find its wicked way with you. You may have noticed when grieving how your mind goes to mush, you cannot concentrate or remember. Your energy plummets as the loss drains you. Your ability to organize and get things done is highly impaired. Therefore, it makes perfect sense that to have to worry about finances, decide whether the deceased wanted to be buried or cremated and to try to find a will would be highly stressful, especially without the resources to handle all of it.

Imagine the huge relief if a dearly beloved person in your life reeling from your loss, would be saved from this drama and stress. It really is the most charitable, loving, kind and generous action that one person can give to those left behind.

*"While I thought that I was learning how to live,
I have been learning how to die."*
~ Leonardo da Vinci

"When my daughter was little I did a meditation called 'A Year To Live'. During this course of living out the year of time as though it were my last, I experienced many intense and profound meditations. During one month, the guided meditation was to have a conversation as though I was dead with all my loved ones I left behind. I was able to fulfill this with everyone apart from my daughter. Yet, when it came to talking with her and explaining I would no longer be there, as her mother, the heartbreak and torture felt too overwhelming.

I knew that I would eventually need to face my fears and fulfill this meditation. Therefore, during my waking hours I pondered what I needed to make the idea of being no longer there for my daughter bearable. The only possible solution was very logical, linear and masculine. Take out a huge life insurance policy. In addition, this is what I did. I also updated my will, talked with dear friends to clarify they would be guardians and set my death in order. The beauty is, many years later, I am still alive and able to mother her. Yet by taking care of her financial and parenting needs as best I could, I relieved some of the terror that even the idea of leaving her ripped through me. I was grateful that there was some kind of solution. I also wrote her a sealed letter that I put in my will telling her how much I deeply loved her and how I would always love her and be there for her even if it was on the spiritual plane."
~ Miranda

WAYS TO MAKE YOUR DEATH AN ACT OF LOVE:

◆ **Write an up-to-date will or living trust.**
Find a reliable and reputable lawyer or estate planner to help guide you through the process. The ones you need will vary depending on whether you have children or not and your own personal situation.

◆ **Be clear about the division of your assets and to whom you wish to leave them.**
This will hopefully limit the possibility of heated arguments by those left behind.

◆ **Choose a trusted person who will become your durable power of attorney.**
This person will have written authorization to represent or act on your behalf in your private affairs, business or other legal matters.

◆ **Decide on your advanced health care directive and appoint a trusted person to make these decisions on your behalf.**
This is also known as a living will and is a set of written instructions that you specify what actions are to be taken surrounding your health if you are no longer able to make decisions due to illness or incapacity.

◆ **Have all your updated deeds to property, belongings and assets in order and easily accessible.**

◆ **Have all your financial details including bank accounts, savings and investments in order, filed and available to a trusted family member so they know where to find these important documents.**

◆ **Write a clear list of all your belongings, itemizing which you want to leave to whom.**
This helps not cause so many issues and conflicts with family members, as they can just blame you!

- Have a copy of your will, living trust, durable power of attorney, advanced health care directives, deeds to property, financial details, personal property transfer and any special instructions filed in a place where your loved ones know where to find these important documents.

- Give a copy of your estate plan to a trusted family member.

- Purchase life insurance.
  This is especially vital if you have young children. It is already a loaded question trying to decide who would be their guardian if something happened to you. Yet the whole scenario is helped if there are plenty of resources to support the transition.

- Make arrangements for and pay for your own funeral.
  This really is a wonderful gift to leave behind.

> *"Life is hard. Then you die.*
> *Then they throw dirt in your face.*
> *Then the worms eat you.*
> *Be grateful it happens in that order."*
> ~ David Gerrold

MONEY SAVING TIPS

As you save, so shall you receive.

*I*n the quest to get your financial affairs in order, it seems appropriate to bring in the time-honored tradition of saving money. Here are some money saving tips to prime the well. The hope is that these suggestions will stimulate you enough to add your own brilliant ideas to the list. As money is saved, you will have more to spend on your heart's true desire!

- **Unplug all electrical devices that do not need to be kept on.**
  It actually costs money to keep them plugged in.

- **Be conscious of turning off lights, which are not needed.**

- **Do not shop when you are hungry or upset.**
  Have you ever noticed how much more you buy when you are in this state?

- **Decide if what you are running is useful, like a second fridge or freezer.**

- **Use blinds to keep the sun out.**

- **Use blankets, sweaters and socks to keep you warm.**

- **Recycle.**

- **Save coins in a container at home.**
  They are heavy to carry around and it does add up!

- **Deal in cash for a while.**
  It is a wakeup call to see the amount of money you are actually spending.

- Go to the cupboard or fridge and find food that you can use to create a meal instead of going to the market.
  You would be amazed at how inventive and creative you can become by having to make a meal out of what you already have.

- Grow your own vegetables.

- Brew your own fancy drinks instead of investing in places like coffee houses.

- Check to see if you actually watch all the channels you are paying for.

- Look into community sharing such as food, travel or anything else that can be bartered.

- Put the phone, internet and cable services under one company's package deal.

- Buy fewer clothes that require dry cleaning.

- Shop around for the best deal.

- Change your light bulbs to energy saving bulbs.

- Use coupons and money-off vouchers.

- Buy in bulk.

- Buy second hand.

- Wash clothes in cold water and hang them outside to dry.

- Use food for your beauty treatments.

- Share your feet or hands with a friend and trade foot or hand rubs.

- Carpool, walk or ride a bike.

- Use scrap paper.

- Color your own hair with a natural hair dye.

- Put a fan by the window at night and turn off the air conditioning.

- If you are redoing your house, you should consider solar panels or weather controlled sprinkler systems.

- Save ten percent of what you earn.

Take care of the pennies and the pounds will take care of themselves.

DEBT IS A FOUR LETTER WORD

Owing, by its very nature drains energy, whether it is time or money. And it leaves you living off someone else's resources with a high price to pay.

Unfortunately, there can be a tendency not to take care of money until desperation sets in. This can also happen with time. Yet both commodities are precious and need to be nurtured as such. As previously mentioned, money is a vehicle that can help you experience and accomplish your dreams. Just as with any tool, if you leave it outside to rust in the rain, the next time you need it, you will be frustrated, as it will no longer work. Money is no different.

Choose to treat it with respect. This can be as simple as keeping your dollar bills in neat piles, rather than crumpled up or picking up loose change and placing it in a bowl.

Debt is another area where your relationship with money can become stressful. The simple mathematics of spending more than you have, will always lead to an imbalance.

When you are in debt, it can cause you to run on your financial adrenals. Never a good resource as many women's adrenals are already fatigued by taking care of everyone else, ignoring your own needs and saying yes when in reality, your heart is crying no.

HERE ARE SOME BASIC RULES REGARDING DEBT:

◆ **Know the difference between a frivolous debt and a wise investment.**
Some debt and borrowing is unavoidable, such as mortgages. The key is to make sure that the servicing of the debt and the interest payments are affordable even if the rates go up. Also, if the opportunity arises to refinance at a better rate, take it.

◆ **Only borrow money as a wise investment.**
Make sure that what you are borrowing the money for will yield a high return. An example of this would be investing in a house, where all due-diligence has been completed and you are reasonably sure of the return. If you are borrowing money to keep you afloat some aspect of your money flow needs to be looked at.

◆ **Avoid running up large credit card bills.**
The rates they charge are punitive and can be unreasonable. Do not put your head in the sand in regards to how much interest you are paying. Chances are you will be able to find a better deal. Always shop around for the lowest interest rate you can find. This particular kind of shopping is highly recommended!

◆ **Do not get into debt in the first place.**
Know how much money you have and keep within that amount. There is a difference between a necessity and an extravagance. Become conscious of this dynamic and choose to stop making irresponsible choices. Shopping is often a quick fix to feel better. As any addiction used to numb feelings, it will eventually backfire when the credit card bill comes. Being responsible around money results in knowing the difference between what you can comfortably afford and what will force you to use someone else's money. If this is the case, it is not yours to buy and you cannot afford it.

◆ **If you receive a windfall of money, consider whether it is right action to pay off your debt.**
This would depend on the interest rate you are paying. If the interest rate is high, paying off the debt makes sense. If the debt has a low interest rate then the chunk of money might be better used elsewhere. Always be aware not to fritter away lumps of money on clothes or accessories. This is easy to do. Always ask the question: What will I have to show for it? It is a blessing and a rare occurrence to receive a large lump of money in your lifetime, such as winnings, inheritances or retirement funds. Make conscious and responsible choices about what to do with these blessings.

- **If you are already in debt, pay it off weekly.**
  Having a debt is like carrying a weight. Therefore, even if you start with just paying off $5 a week toward the money you owe, over time the debt will decrease and the stress and weight of it will lessen. If at any time you can pay off more once your basics are covered, see this as an opportunity to release the debt faster and to clean your slate.

- **Always know how much you owe.**
  If you owe someone money you are indebted to them energetically as well as materially. This can be disempowering. It is much cleaner to be debt-free or to pay off your debt consistently, however small the amount.

- **Keep in touch with the person you are indebted to.**
  Even if it is to let them know that you will not be able to pay until the following month.

- **Keep your credit score as high as possible.**
  Property owners and employers now check credit scores. A high score will also afford you a better interest rate when taking out a loan and give you more choices. Therefore, it is vital to do everything necessary to elevate your score. Be careful not to check your score too frequently, as this can affect your rating.

F**K YOU MONEY

what every woman needs.

During this time of accessing your Feminine Power, it seems vital for every woman to know she has some money of her own.

In the unfortunate event that you ever need to leave a situation, whether it be a relationship, a home, a job or even a country, it is crucial you have the resources available to protect and provide for your own well-being. This enables you to know that you have a primary way of providing a sense of security and freedom for you and your loved ones. Whenever there is a dependency on someone else, there is a loss of power. By having your own private stash of money you are empowering yourself and ultimately giving yourself freedom of choice.

ACCUMULATING F**K YOU MONEY:

◆ This money should be set aside in a private account.
  This could be a trust fund, a safety deposit box or placed somewhere discreet.

◆ Label the money as 'Self-Care', giving it a positive intention.

◆ Add to the money on a regular basis so it keeps growing.

◆ This money will give you a sense of stability and security, like a safety net.

◆ No one needs to know about this money or how much there is.

◆ Whenever you feel stressed about money, remind yourself you have this nest egg and know that this is an ultimate act of self-love.

This money is your business, your investment,
your freedom and your sanctuary.

EXPAND MONEY CONSCIOUSNESS
No more retail therapy.

Many women get a kick out of shopping, some more than others! It can be a highly effective way to numb an unpleasant feeling, or give yourself a reward. Buying for yourself can also be a tool to break the cycle of giving too much to others and shifting that dynamic back to giving to yourself.

Yet, have you ever noticed how sometimes the thrill comes from the actual purchase and not necessarily from the use of the item itself. In this situation, it is immaterial whether you actually walk out of the store with the acquisition.

For those of you who get more of a rush out of the shopping experience rather than owning the actual object, it is crucial to inquire into why you are buying an item in the first place. You will know this is the case if you own clothes or shoes that you have never actually worn and still have the tags on them!

While you are on this journey of cleaning up your money awareness, it is vital to know when you use spending as a form of therapy or reward. This can be online, from catalogs or shopping in person. Pay particular attention if your finances are in the red. It is then essential to take some time and to discover if there is a healthier form of therapy that would serve you better and hopefully one that is free. If you know you are feeling emotional and in need of some nurturing, often a hot bath or a good night's sleep can do the trick. Obviously, this is not quite as dramatic or as aesthetically appealing as a new pair of shoes, yet the result is that your bank account, credit cards and overall well-being will reap the benefits.

Both shopping and food can have the same numbing yet intoxicating effect. Just as with any drug, they feel satisfying and filling in the moment, yet the aftermath can be ugly, life altering and can cause long-term damage.

"I always keep a hundred dollar bill in my wallet. Periodically it is spent, but I did have one particular bill that lasted two years, yet I spent it in my mind hundreds of times. As I shop or look through catalogues and see something that appeals to me, I say to myself 'I can buy that. I have the money.' In that moment I feel free and receive that lovely little energy jolt we get from spending. In reality, I usually choose not to buy the object." ~ *Miranda*

Imagine having a never-ending virtual one hundred dollar bill or two if need be. This feeling is free and without the credit card bill at the end of the month. Or take it a step further and physically place some bills in a section of your wallet and have fun hypothetically spending to your heart's content. This scenario is very different to seeing something you want to buy and continuously telling yourself that you cannot afford it or buying it anyway even though it is beyond your budget.

A good question to ask is:

Will this purchase enhance all aspects of my life?

Then wait for an honest response.

Often the hundred dollar bill will remain in your wallet, as you realize the purchase was not a necessity or prudent at the time.

Surprisingly, this practice can actually strengthen the fabric of your money consciousness. If you tend to over-save, it will increase your flow of money as you imagine all the different places you can spend. If you tend to over-spend, it will decrease your debt and help you develop more awareness around any money hemorrhaging. Either way, the attention you give to your finances is expanded.

DOUBLE YOUR MONEY

An exercise to break through the bonds of your money consciousness.

Imagine being given a thousand dollars in this moment. Chances are you would probably know exactly what you would want to do with it.

Yet if you already had everything material you could wish for and someone gave you a hundred million dollars, apart from giving it away or investing, it can actually become a quandary as to how to spend it all.

"This is a brilliant exercise. I have done it many times and am still in awe that you can actually get to a point where you have so much money to spend that it boggles your mind as what to do with it! This may be rather telling why many of us are not outrageously rich." ~ Miranda

This exercise makes you think outside the box and amplifies your imaginative capacity for spending. By expanding your horizons and allowing your dreams to unfold fully, you will no longer be limited by your restrictive beliefs around money.

THE EXERCISE IS SIMPLE:

◆ On the 'Double Your Money Diary', list 'day one' in the far left column.

◆ Record the amount you are going to spend in the middle column, beginning with $1,000.00.

◆ To the right, imagine what you would spend the day's allocation of money on and write it down. Be very specific.

◆ Next write down a rough estimate of what each item would cost.

◆ Double the amount of money each day and write out exactly what the money is spent on.

◆ The only rule is you must spend all the money for that day.

Be inventive, imaginative, generous and have fun!

The follow is an example of the Double Your Money Diary:

DAY:	AMOUNT TO SPEND:	COST:	PURCHASE:
Day 1	$1,000.00	$300.00	fix computer
		$100.00	massage
		$300.00	clothes and underwear
		$200.00	orthotics
		$100.00	favorite charity
Day 2	$2,000.00	$2000.00	college fund
Day 3	$4,000.00	$2,000.00	tankless water heater
		$2,000.00	new bathtub
Day 4	$8,000.00	$8,000.00	fix roof, plumbing and electrical
Day 5	$16,000.00	$5000.00	family vacation
		$10,000.00	property taxes
		$1000.00	gift to daughter
Day 6	$32,000.00	$10,000.00	pay off debt
		$10,000.00	college fund
		$10,000.00	business investment
		$2,000.00	charity
Day 7	$64,000.00	$10,000.00	college fund
		$10,000.00	business investment
		$11,000.00	charity
		$10,000.00	gift to Mum
		$10,000.00	gift to daughter
		$10,000.00	home improvement
		$3,000.00	outrageous fun
Day 8	$128,000.00	$100,000.00	house principal
		$12,000.00	charity
		$8,000.00	college fund
		$8,000.00	another vacation!

DOUBLE YOUR MONEY DIARY

Living in virtual abundance.

DAY: AMOUNT TO SPEND: COST: PURCHASE:

THE MONEY POT
Growing your own money.

Money consciousness is a key factor in creating a financial freedom 'buffer-zone' between you, and the outside world. Having financial autonomy allows you to expand and grow without outside restrictions or limitations imposed upon you. This important and vital concept of using a money pot as a way to expand your money consciousness is inspired by the following question:

If you could choose between being given one million dollars in cash today or one cent put into a bank account, that doubles the amount of the previous day everyday for one year, which one would you choose?

At first, the cash looked highly inviting, but when you pause a moment you may realize that the one-cent doubled for 365 days would actually be much more! In fact by the end of the year you would have an unpronounceable amount of money.

"So I decided to give it a try. I placed a glass mason jar on the counter in the money corner of my house and began saving. On Day Eighteen, a miracle occurred. I needed a certain amount of money to get my book re-printed and I was short. After sitting for a moment, a thought popped into my head to count the money in the jar. It added up to the amount I was missing, minus a dollar or two. I used the money, giving deep thanks that I had put it aside and started the jar again with one cent."
~ Miranda

For what will you choose to save?

HERE IS THE PRACTICE:

◆ **Set a positive intention for the money's use.**
Never save for a rainy day, because eventually whatever you save for will happen. Therefore, in this case, you will get a rainy day and have to spend your hard-earned savings on some disaster. Instead, save for self-care desires such as home improvements or a vacation.

◆ **Find a clean jar or container.**

◆ **Place it in the money corner of your room or home.**
There are two very simple ways to find the money corner: As you walk in the door, the far left hand corner of the space is the money and abundance section. Imagine dividing the space into nine equal segments and the far left segment is where to place your pot. The other option is to enhance the South West corner of your home or room, as this direction is in alignment with prosperity.

◆ **On day one, add one cent.**

◆ **On day two, add two cents.**

◆ **On day three, add four cents.**

◆ **Keep doubling the quantity until you can no longer meet the doubled amount.**
Stretch a little, but always take care of your essential survival needs first.

◆ **When you have completed one jar, leave it until it is time to spend it on the intention you set for yourself.**

◆ **Then start a new jar with a new intention and follow the same steps.**
The second jar can also be a continuation of the first jar's intention. This can happen when you reach a number that is too big to stuff into the jar!

◆ You can have as many jars as you like lined up, but keep only one active.

"What I found was each time I started a new jar I could stretch a little further with the amount. Oddly enough, I thoroughly looked forward to putting the money in each day, or figuring out a way to make it possible. As we know, money is energy so by placing this extremely clear intention, the universe seemed to respond and every time I saw my jars, I felt richer, which was obviously a good feeling!" ~ Miranda

REVEAL MORE TRUTH

A rich opportunity to inquiry into self-worth and finances.

As you notice any dysfunctional behaviors surrounding money, do not fret.

It is much better to know that you have been making strange unconscious choices and that you are now choosing to become aware. This will keep you from flailing around in the dark, desperately hoping for something to change.

Remember, if it feels as though you have found yourself in the thick of a dark forest when it comes to your relationship with money, you now have the tools and direction to find your way.

You always have a choice. You will be spending this time delving around for your light switch, finding it and turning it on. It is up to you whether you keep this light of consciousness alive or you plunge yourself back into darkness again.

Growth always requires movement.

THIS MEANS, YOU ARE REVEALING MORE TRUTH:

◆ **Read through the written text.**

◆ **Complete your 'Revealing Money Chart.'**
Be sure to account for every penny for your own clarity. This will empower you beyond measure. To print your own copy, go here:
www.MirandaJBarrett.com/resources/the-abundance-of-wealth.

◆ **Choose at least one activity or exercise from the writings.**
Have fun exploring your relationship with money.

- **Come up with at least three plans of action regarding your money situation.**
  One could be as simple as knowing you need more money or the realization that you need to do more detailed work regarding shifts in your money expenditures. For example, 'I will no longer spend $20.00 a week on coffee'.

- **Be mindful of your most limiting beliefs around money.**
  Use 'The Bond Between Money and Fear' exercise from the writings to find yourself a new and juicier belief that will support an abundant and prosperous life.

- **Live in gratitude to cultivate your dreams and desires into manifestation.**
  As you delve into the world of gratitude, notice any impulse or inclination to thank someone. This may be a situation from the past or a present day. Either way, it is never too late to express gratitude. To write a thank you card or to express in person how much someone's actions meant to you is priceless.

The goal here is to live an abundant life. The definition of abundance is an extremely plentiful or over sufficient quantity or supply. The more clarity you lend to your finances, the more abundance you will realize.

An analogy for this is, clearing out a closet. You can feel abundant as you uncover items you did not know you had and still love. By clearing out the junk, which is a symbol for old distorted beliefs, you make a space for new and improved items. When it comes to the closet of the mind, it is all about changing your thoughts. The good news is that you do not even need a truck to haul them away!

It is literally all about changing your mind.

May this be a time of abundance in all areas of your life
including money, gifts, love, gratitude and anything your heart desires.

Wishing you all the integrity you need to live in your truth and prosperity,

With Love,

Miranda

THE HAPPINESS EQUATION
Happiness vs misery

Once you have accurately disphered your monthly outgoings,
it is time to measure it against your income.
Be courageous and loving with yourself. It is simply mathmatics, which does not lie.
This will give you the vital information to either heave a sigh of relief
or adjust your financial world so you are able to breath again!

INCOME   —   OUTGOING   =   HAPPINESS / MISERY

$
$
$
$
$

Total: $ Total: $ + Total: $ − Total: $

Copyright 2011 A Woman's Truth

CHARTS, CHARTS, GLORIOUS CHARTS

"Deadly Sin: Wealth without work, pleasure without conscience, science without humanity, commerce without reality."
~Gandhi

This Revealing Money Chart will bring a whole new level of awareness and consciousness to your habits and the foundations of your financial being, and will give you clarity beyond measure on what is working in your world and what is not.

◆ Please go to **www.MirandaJBarrett.com/resources/abundance-of-wealth** to print out more copies of The Happiness Equation and A Revealing Money Chart for yourself. Give yourself the gift of financial clarity laid out in front of you.

◆ Take this next month to fill out A Revealing Money Chart. Be as accurate as possible, even if you do not know the exact amounts. Any amount is more accurate than no amount!

◆ Leave the chart out somewhere accessible so you can document your spending quickly and easily. Pay attention to your bills, checks, credit cards and even cash.

◆ Once you have figured out your monthly outgoings, it is time to fill out **The Happiness Equation**. Meditate on The Happiness Equation until you see your patterns and how you can shift them to an abundant wealth frequency.

◆ Ask yourself the powerful question: Is your relationship with money giving you vital energy or is it taking energy away?

◆ Once you are clear about your basic money needs and see the importance of honoring this vital aspect of your life, make the necessary adjustments to lovingly replenish and nurture yourself.

◆ Once you have discovered how to be abundantly filled financially, you are now ready to build upon that foundation daily.

A REVEALING MONEY CHART

Use this chart as a way to monitor your daily, weekly and monthly spending. Be as accurate as possible.

MONTH:

Rent/Mortgage	$	Drinking Water	$	Hair Care / Hair Removal	$
Property Tax	$	Drinks	$	Body Care / Body Work	$
Home Owners Insurance	$	Vehicles	$	Massage / Facial / Nails	$
Home Owners Association	$	Payment	$	Make Up / Creams	$
Bank Fees / Safe Deposit Box	$	Insurance	$	Exercise	$
Interest on Debt	$	Registration	$	Classes / Trainers	$
Paying off Debt	$	Maintenance	$	Equipment	$
Utilities	$	Gas / Parking	$	Clothes / Shoes	$
Gas	$	Medical	$	Shoe Repair	$
Water	$	Dental	$	Tailoring / Laundry Service	$
Electric	$	Optical	$	Jewelry / Accessories / Bags	$
Trash	$	Medical Bills	$	Subscriptions / Books / Magazines	$
Cable / Video Streaming	$	Medication / Supplements	$	Electronics / Computers / Media	$
Internet	$	Therapy	$	Entertainment / Hobbies	$
Phones / Cell Phones	$	Child Care	$	Movies / DVD's / CD's	$
Burglar Alarm	$	Education / College Fund	$	Concerts / Theater / Parks	$
Home Repair /	$	Tutors / Day Care	$	Sports	$

Maintenance					
Furniture	$	Allowance	$	Travel / Vacation	$
Household Decorations	$	Alimony	$	Gifts / Holidays / Christmas	$
Household Supplies	$	Animals	$	Postage / PO Box	$
House Keeper	$	Food	$	Taxes / Accounting	$
Window Cleaner	$	Vet / Boarding	$	Legal Fees	$
Pool Maintenance	$	Grooming / Accessories	$	Savings / Investments	$
Gardener	$	Insurance	$	Health Insurance	$
Gardening Supplies	$	Spiritual Study / Purchases	$	Life Insurance	$
Food	$	Education / Self Study	$	Retirement	$
Groceries	$	Workshops / Retreats	$	Charity / Donations	$
Eating Out	$	Beautifying Procedures	$	**TOTAL**	$

**Please go to
www.MirandaJBarrett.com/resources/the-abundance-of-wealth
to print out more copies for yourself.**

ABOUT MIRANDA
A spirited guide and mentor.

Miranda is a passionate and devoted leader. Her loving and wise support will guide you on a transformational journey as her powerful teachings unveil the truth of who you are. Her gift is to offer potent tools, which inspire exquisite and beautiful self-care and empower you to live the fullest and most authentic life possible. As a mentor and guide, Miranda deeply walks her talk and is fearless about her own path of self-discovery, as she weaves the sacred into the mundane.

The simple, yet powerful premise offered by the mystic Rumi is the foundation of Miranda's philosophy and mission:

> *"Never give from the depths of your well,
> always give from your overflow."*

Miranda gives Council and Guidance for the Mind, Body and Spirit. With a background in Nutrition and Energy work, Miranda is the Creator of 'A Woman's Truth' and 'The Spirit of Energy', an Author, a Workshop and Retreat Leader, a Reiki Master and Yoga and Meditation teacher. Miranda studies under the guidance of her Beloved teachers Rod Stryker and Adyashanti.

To speak with or follow Miranda, please call or visit:

Phone: 626~798~6544
eMail: Info@MirandaJBarrett.com
Website: www.MirandaJBarrett.com
Facebook: Miranda J Barrett
Twitter: MirandaJBarrett

ABOUT HELEN
visionary artist.

Helena Nelson-Reed is a visionary artist whose primary medium is watercolor. Born in Seattle, Washington, she was raised in Marin County and Napa Valley, California and today lives in Illinois. A largely self taught artist whose educational emphasis and degree is in psychology, Nelson-Reed's primary focus is exploring the collective consciousness and the portrayal of archetypal imagery in the tradition of Carl Jung and Joseph Campbell. Rendered in luminous watercolor technique often described as ephemeral, Nelson-Reed's paintings are created in extraordinary detail, pushing the medium of watercolor past the usual limits. Her work may be found in private collections, book covers, magazines and cd covers. Nelson-Reed also has a line of jewelry, calendars and greeting cards.

Helena's Mission:

My images can be interpreted many ways, and for some will serve as portal to the mythic landscape. Descriptions providing background about each painting are available by request. Navigating and translating myth into contemporary wisdom is the traditional way of transmitting information though a shamanic and multi-cultural practice.

Myth, fairy, folk and spiritual lore describe divine beings and supernatural life forms arriving unbidden and disguised. In our earthly dimension, mortals often play similar roles in the lives of one another. Destinies and energies collide and interact, visible and invisible forces are at work. The mythic realms are timeless, offering insight and inspiration. While my paintings have a positive energy, many have roots in the shadows of life experience and human psyche; like the lotus blossom rooted in pond mud. For many, life is one challenge followed by the next, like beads on an endless string.

Take heart! Like goddess Inanna, one may navigate the underworld, move through dark places yet return to the realms of light battle scarred but wiser, richer for the experience. Read the ancient tales, the great mythic literature; draw strength, for they are repositories of wisdom.

Visit Helena's website for her art, purchase information and art to wear jewelry:

eMail: HNelsonReed@Gmail.com
Websites: www.HelenaNelsonReed.com
www.etsy.com/shop/HelenaNelsonReed
Blog: www.dancingdovestudio.blogspot.com
Facebook: MorningDove Design By Helena

MIRANDA'S WORLD

*Ways to stay connected
and aligned with your truth.*

BOOKS:

A Woman's Truth
A life truly worth living.

Priceless teachings reveal your transformational
journey ahead. Obstacles to self care are explored
as clear and loving intentions are conceived.

The Grandeur Of Sleep
Permission to rest.

Miraculous benefits are realized as the worlds of sleep,
relaxation and rejuvenation are explored and deeply honored.

Nourishing Nutrition
Reclaim your health and vitality.

Reap the bountiful rewards while eating as nature intended.
Claim your health and vitality with these simple,
yet powerful tools to nourish and heal your body.

Embodying Movement
Ground your whole being.

Discover how to embrace your whole being
through the life-enhancing benefits of body movement.

Body Care
Cherish your body as a temple.

Learn to honor your extraordinary body
as a living temple and listen to the healing messages she whispers.

Feminine Power
Fully access your supreme birthright.

Welcome and reclaim this intrinsic privilege while living
in harmonious balance between the masculine and the feminine.

The Abundance Of Wealth
Receive the gifts of prosperity.

Understand the energy flow of prosperity and weave
the threads of abundance throughout the tapestry of your life.

Find Your Authentic Voice
The courage to express who you truly are.

Your greatest ally is born
when you courageously speak your truth and claim your unique power.

Loving Yourself
A love affair with the self.

As you become highly attuned to your own needs,
allow love to lead the way. Grant yourself permission
to honor and express your heart's truest desires.
Love yourself, no matter what.

Living A Spiritual Life
Ground your divinity here on earth.

Discover what spirituality means to you, by consciously
living between the two worlds of the sacred and the mundane.

Service As A Way Of Life
Ignite the fire of love to truly be of service.

By utilizing the gems of exquisite self care
on a daily basis and honoring your truth, your mission of service is born.

The Crowning Glory
Fully Rejoice in Being You.

A celebration overflowing with love,
blessings, grace and gratitude. Stand confident within
your own truth as your mind becomes of service to your heart.

The Food of Life
The versatile vegetable.

More than just a cookbook,
a comprehensive guide for nourishing your life.

Reiki
The spirit of Energy.

An insightful guidebook full of wisdom
which introduces you to the potent and healing world of Reiki.

CARDS:

Inspiration Cards
A daily Spiritual Practice.

Sixty-Five cards with simple yet inspirational qualities
to live by and an insightful guidebook to lead the way.

CD'S:

The Grandeur of Sleep and Rejuvenating Rest

An ancient healing art of rest and relaxation.

Simple yet profound practices, which alleviate stress and tension allowing your mind, body and spirit to heal, restore and replenish.

TO ORDER PLEASE VISIT:

www.MirandaJBarrett.com
www.Amazon.com

All books are available in printed or eBook form.

TESTIMONIES
to 'A Woman's Truth' teachings.

"There are no words to describe every experience with Miranda. She is a wonderful person to be around and a master at her work. I am very grateful to have her in my life and know that no matter what life has planned, she will always be there with her positive spirit and guidance."

Jasmine ~ Ear Honing ~ Monrovia, CA

"Miranda inspires with her passionate love of health, healing, awakening and embodiment. She is an extremely resourced teacher who shares her wisdom and knowledge with integrity, gentleness and humor. In her books she holds a grounded safe space, enabling women to share their vulnerabilities and embrace their personal truths."

Leah ~ RPP ~ Altadena, CA

"Miranda is a Worthy and Present Guide! She has a voice and message of crystal clarity, and an authentic, loving nature. I always feel seen, heard and understood by her from the heart. She is also a bright leader who knows herself and her purpose, and I deeply admire her commitment to her work. She inspires me to be my best and I am grateful for her."

Stacey ~ Reiki Master ~ Santa Barbara, CA

"Once I began honoring 'The Foundational Trinity' of getting enough sleep, eating well and exercising regularly, my life literally changed! I feel calmer, happier, more energized and so less stressed. It seems the gift of 'A Woman's Truth' books keeps on giving."

Zoe ~ Mother ~ La Cañada, CA

www.ingramcontent.com/pod-product-compliance
Lightning Source LLC
Chambersburg PA
CBHW080520110426
42742CB00017B/3182